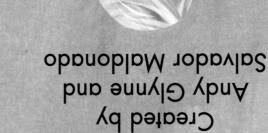

# SUMMER'S
## STORY

Living with Epilepsy

Created by
Andy Glynne and
Salvador Maldonado

FRANKLIN WATTS
LONDON • SYDNEY

Franklin Watts
First published in Great Britain in 2017 by The Watts Publishing Group

Mosaic Films, Shacklewell Lane, London E8 2EZ

Created by Nandita Jain and Andy Glynne

Editor: Sarah Silver

ISBN 978 1 4451 5666 8

Printed in China

Franklin Watts
An imprint of
Hachette Children's Group
Part of The Watts Publishing Group
Carmelite House
50 Victoria Embankment
London EC4Y 0DZ

An Hachette UK Company
www.hachette.co.uk
www.franklinwatts.co.uk

My name is Summer and I have epilepsy.

Epilepsy is ...

I don't want to say

it's a 'DISABILITY' ...

for me it's just

# AN OBSTACLE.

or if there's really, really bright lights and I look up at them, I go into a full-blown seizure.

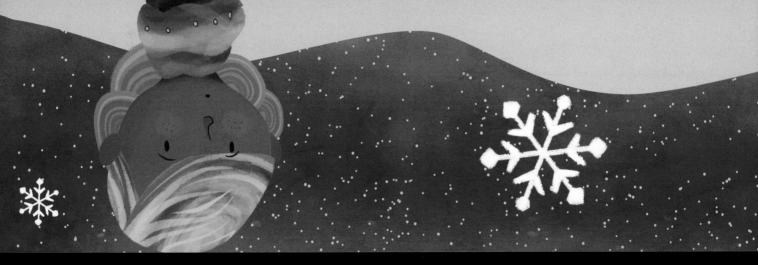

or if I get too COLD,

If I get too HOT

I get a seizure because of something that goes off in my BRAIN. The brain is sending electrical messages all the time.

A seizure happens if the messages are interrupted, or if there is a sudden BURST of intense electrical activity in the brain.

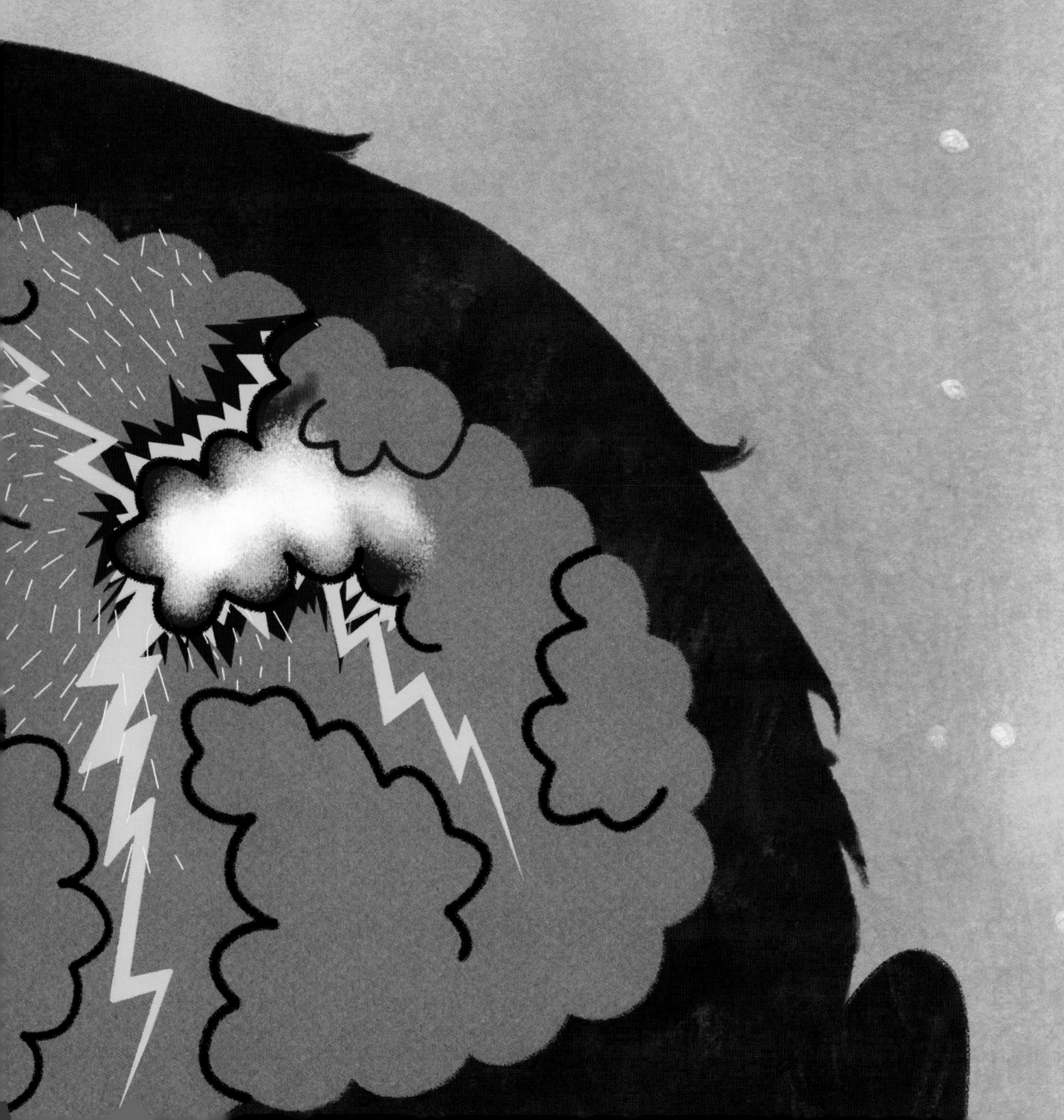

An ABSENCE SEIZURE can happen ...

anytime,

anywhere,

and I'm not aware that they've actually happened.

They can go for ten, maybe fifteen seconds.
It's sort of like I'm staring into space,
like there's nothing there except for me looking at thin air.

I can't hear and I can't speak. I don't even blink.

I know I'm there, but I don't feel like I'm there.
It sort of feels like someone is filling in for me.

I come around and I don't remember what's going on, what's been said or who's written what on the board.

I think it really, really affects my grades.

I usually get told off
quite a lot in lessons
because it looks like
I'm not concentrating.

I've tried to explain to teachers,
but they just don't listen.
It doesn't give me a lot
of confidence.

Another type of seizure
is called a TONIC CLONIC.
They can happen when I'm ill
or when I'm in the middle of
watching a film.

A TONIC CLONIC lasts longer
than an ABSENCE SEIZURE.
It's a full-blown spasm.

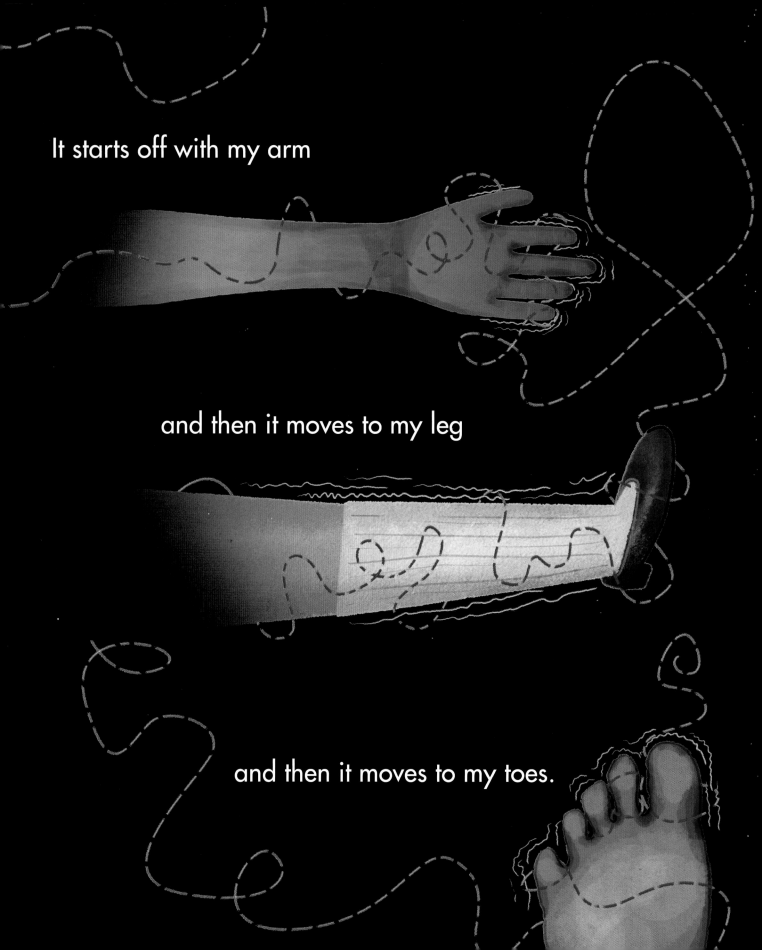

It starts off with my arm

and then it moves to my leg

and then it moves to my toes.

As soon as I go to talk, it's like i'm MUTE
and my voice box doesn't work.

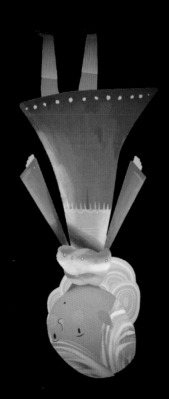

I can hear but I can't speak.

A lot of people are afraid of asking me to go around to their house.

They are scared they won't know what to do
if I have a seizure.

I feel really jealous and upset when my friends tell me they've been to see a film in 3D.

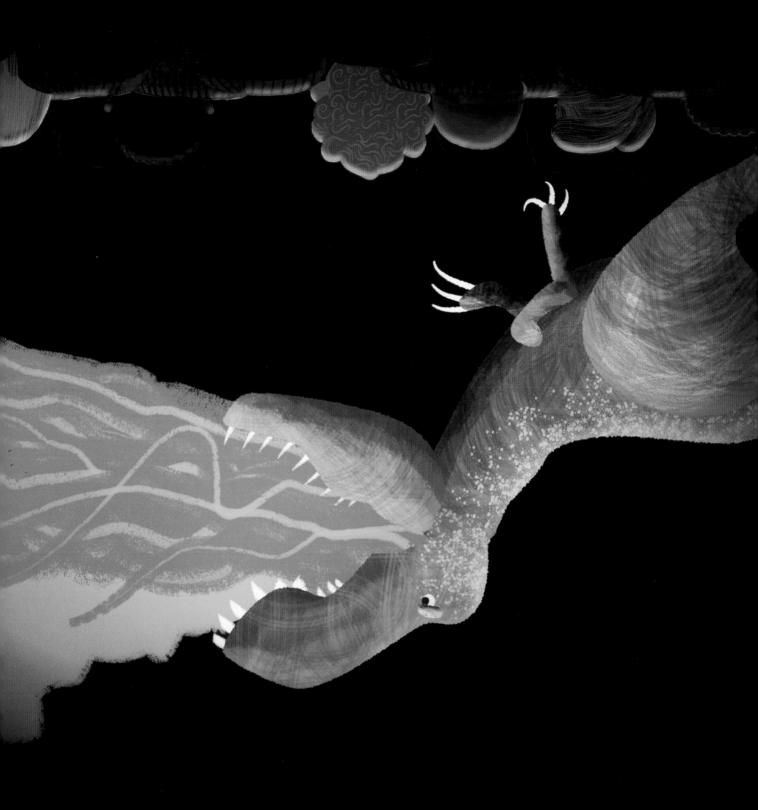

If I did see a 3D movie, it would bring on a seizure.

My mum comes on school trips
because she has to give me medication.

I feel embarrassed that my mum is there.
I love my mum, but sometimes there's that little bit of me
that wants her not to be there.

When I'm at home and I'm writing
stories and plays, I feel HAPPY.

When I go to school,
I feel like I'm playing another person.

I don't feel like I'm me.

I sometimes think 'why does it have to be me?'
But I know, if I want to act like a miserable person
I can act like a miserable person.

And what's the point of that when
I have got my whole life ahead of me?

# FURTHER INFORMATION ABOUT EPILEPSY

Epilepsy is a neurological condition that disrupts the normal electrical activity our brains use to communicate with the rest of the body. Sometimes a doctor might be able to advise on what may have caused epilepsy, however, in around 60 per cent of cases a specific cause is not found. Epilepsy often develops during childhood but can develop at any age.

### What is an epileptic seizure?

A seizure is a sudden episode of electrical activity in the brain that can cause involuntary muscle movements or changes in sensation, behaviour or consciousness. Seizures can take many forms because the brain is responsible for such a wide range of the body's function. There are in fact over 40 different types of seizure. Most seizures usually last from a few seconds to a few minutes and stop without any treatment. Some may go on for longer and medication may be needed to stop them.

### Triggers

Epilepsy affects each person differently and there is a wide range of potential seizure triggers. Some of the more common triggers include tiredness, stress and overexcitement. Contrary to popular belief, only around 5 per cent of people with epilepsy are sensitive to flashing or flickering lights. There is not always a clear trigger for seizures and they can often occur without warning.

### What can be done?

People with epilepsy take medicine to help prevent seizures. Sometimes doctors perform an operation on the part of the brain that the seizures originate from. For some people, a special diet can also help to prevent seizures. In day-to-day life, people try to avoid known triggers and situations that could be dangerous, should they have a seizure. It is important for friends and family and those in the person's community to learn about epilepsy, how it can affect people and what to do if a seizure occurs.

For more information and resources, visit youngepilepsy.org.uk.
For support and information, contact the Young Epilepsy Helpline
on 01342 831342 or email helpline@youngepilepsy.org.uk.

# The complete Living with... series.
# Real-life testimonies of children living with illness.

978 14451 5604 0

978 14451 5666 8

978 14451 5662 0

978 14451 5668 2

978 14451 5664 4

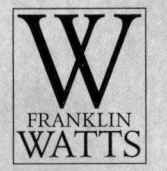

FRANKLIN WATTS

www.franklinwatts.co.uk